EUROPA ⎮ MILITARIA
SPECIAL Nº16

CONFEDERATE TROOPS
of the
American Civil War

Jonathan Sutherland

THE CROWOOD PRESS

First published in 2005 by
The Crowood Press Ltd
Ramsbury, Marlborough
Wiltshire SN8 2HR

www.crowood.com

British Library Cataloguing-in-Publication Data
A catalogue record for this book is available from the British
Library.

ISBN 1 86126 768 1

Contents

Typeset by Jean Cussons Typesetting, Diss, Norfolk

Printed and bound in Singapore by Craft Print International

Introduction

AT the beginning of the American Civil War (1861–5), with the exception of the small regular army of the United States, the vast majority of soldiers went into battle as members of the states' militias, dressed in the pre-war uniforms of those units. Some were wearing clothing that dated back to the war against Mexico (1846–8), while many Confederates simply wore their civilian clothing along with their military equipment.

The Confederate regiments were as diverse as was possible, with regiments composed of companies of militia from across the state, and each company dressed in different clothing. Initially this caused a great deal of confusion on the battlefield as, for example, Confederate National Guard regiments from Alabama were dressed in Yankee blue, while New York National Guard regiments wore all grey uniforms. Almost universally Confederate officers, recently discharged from the Federal army, wore their blue uniforms.

After the first battle of Bull Run (Manassas) in July 1861, it became clear that this first major campaign was not going to decide the outcome of the war, as had previously been expected. Both the Confederacy and the Union began to confront the economic reality of equipping their troops. Dress regulations were laid down and both sides sought cheap suppliers of uniforms – a false economy, as many of the shoddy uniforms disintegrated in wet weather. The Confederate Government never drew up elaborate dress regulations, the responsibility for clothing the troops falling to the states of their origin. North Carolina issued excellent-quality uniforms to its men, but refused to supply other states. At the end of the war 50,000 non-issued uniforms were found in North Carolina's state warehouses, which would have been sufficient to dress the entire Army of Northern Virginia.

As the war dragged on, the best quartermaster that the Confederacy ever had was the Federal Government. Rebels wore many items of Yankee clothing, including their much-prized shoes and sky-blue trousers. The net consequence of the states' responsibility to clothe their own men was that the majority of the regiments took on a ragamuffin appearance. In any regiment or company the clothing would be as varied as the men. They wore a variety of short jackets, usually with standing collars and single rows of buttons. Plain trousers of various colours were usual, as was the peaked cap. Officers tended to wear either short jackets or frock coats.

For the most part, regiments were either disinterested or simply failed to comply with the dress regulations that had been issued on 6 June 1861. The average soldier was at least issued with virtually everything he needed when he first enlisted, but the rigours of a life on campaign meant that the soldiers had to make do and mend, as there was little opportunity for re-supply. According to the regulations each soldier was to have been issued with two jackets during his first year of enlistment, and three pairs of trousers. In practical terms, however, the men were lucky to receive a re-issue every six months.

An average pair of trousers would last just a month and a jacket three months. An average infantryman would have a selection of shirts, a hat, a jacket, underclothing, at least one pair

A re-enactor depicting the legendary Confederate Commander of the Army of Northern Virginia, Robert E. Lee. Lee resigned his commission in the US Army in April 1861 and pledged his allegiance primarily to his native state of Virginia in the hope that his allegiance would restore peace to the United States. 'Uncle Robert' as he became known, led the Confederates during the Battle of the Seven Days, Second Bull Run, South Mountain, Harper's Ferry, Antietam, Fredericksburg, Chancellorsville, Gettysburg, the Wilderness Campaign and the battles around Richmond and Petersburg, before finally surrendering at Appomattox Court House in April 1865. Lee is depicted here in his dress uniform, with his general's stars on the collar of his jacket. Lee's family home was seized during the war and later became part of Arlington National Cemetery. He died in Lexington, Virginia in October 1870. His application for the restoration of his citizenship was not granted until the 1970s.

of trousers, several pairs of socks and a pair of shoes. The majority of the clothing was made of wool. It was originally intended that the men would be issued with cotton clothing for spring and summer campaigns, while the woollen clothing would be reserved for autumn and winter operations.

The average infantryman carried a load of around 40lb (18kg). This would include his waist belt, a pouch for his percussion caps, a second pouch for his cartridges (the former worn on the hip and the latter either on the hip, waist belt or on a sling over the shoulder), a leather scabbard for his bayonet, a canvas haversack and a water bottle. Every man also had a blanket roll, usually slung from his left shoulder to his right hip. Many carried cooking gear and, above all, each had his rifled musket.

As the war drew on, any semblance of uniform began to disappear. Men would wear a variety of hats, different-length jackets of differing composition, and a huge variety of trousers, shoes and boots. If the men were lucky they would have some form of waterproof with them, which could either be used as a groundsheet or be wrapped around them in poor weather.

As the cavalry considered themselves to be an elite force, many of them tried to obtain yellow material for their facings (infantry wore blue facings and artillery, red). Again, their equipment varied: some of them looked like little more than armed civilians while others retained their regulation frock coats or short jackets. Kepis were frequently worn, but more commonly a broad-brimmed hat was favoured.

The artillery tended to have regulation frock coats or short jackets, with red facings in each case. Generally speaking, the men carried a haversack and water bottle, together with a revolver, with a pouch for caps and a box for cartridges. Most of the men, at one stage or another, would have been issued with a sabre, but many discarded this weapon.

This book and its companion, *EMS17 – Union Troops of the American Civil War*, depict British-based re-enactors of the American Civil War Society. This is the largest American Civil War re-enactment group outside the USA. They currently have nearly 1,000 regular re-enactors representing, on the Confederate side, units from Tennessee, Virginia, South and North Carolina, Maryland, Texas and Louisiana. Their website is www.acws.co.uk and their postal address ACWS, PO Box 52, Brighouse, West Yorkshire, HD6 1JQ.

Confederate infantry in a variety of government issue grey uniforms and state-provided garments. Note the variety of different flags, including the state flag to the right and variations of the Confederate 'Stars and Bars' to the left. The mounted Confederate officer wears a slouch hat and sack coat, and has a long cavalry sabre, which appears to be attached to the front of his saddle. The infantry have adopted characteristic linear firing lines to engage the enemy and are advancing in measured rushes to close the ground between them and the Union infantry.

Infantry Officers

ACCORDING to General Order 4, issued on 6 June 1861, all Confederate officers were instructed to wear double-breasted grey tunics. The tunic was to extend to halfway between the hip and the knee. The jacket was to have seven buttons on the front, three buttons each on the cuffs, and four buttons on the back and skirt. The standard jacket was also to have a standing collar with the rank insignia. A second lieutenant was to have a single, half-inch gold bar, a first lieutenant two gold bars and a captain three gold bars. A major was to be identified by a single gold star, with a lieutenant colonel having two and a colonel having three. The cuffs were to display a gold braid design known as the Austrian knot: a lieutenant was to have a single braid, a captain two and field officers three. Due to the tendency for both sides to pick off officers, by mid-1862 officers were allowed to wear fatigue dress on the battlefield without their collar insignia.

(**Right**) Standard officer jacket in cadet grey. This uniform has US Army-style shoulder straps and a stand-up collar. The officer wears a buckle plate, denoting service in the Eastern Theatre of the war. The officer was likely to carry a British Beaumont-Adams revolver in a holster attached to his belt. The uniform depicts an officer of a Virginian regiment, as indicated by the black epaulettes and facing. The cap badge is probably taken from a US Army infantry officer's cap, which were occasionally worn by Confederate officers.

An infantry major in a frock coat. This double-breasted coat has a second row of buttons. In addition to his pistol, the officer is carrying what is probably a Model 1860 cavalry sabre. He is carrying his own personal equipment in a haversack and shoulder bag. He has an oval CSA Eastern Theatre buckle plate and has opted for a civilian-style hat.

(Below) A pair of infantry officers, armed with pistols and sabres. Note the coloration difference between the uniforms. The officer on the right has opted for the standard cadet grey, while the officer on the left has a buff, almost butternut-coloured uniform. The officer on the left has what appears to be civilian clothing adapted for military use. Both wear broad-brimmed hats, much favoured by Confederate officers. Both officers carry haversacks and the one in the buff uniform has a waterproof leather backpack for his personal belongings.

(Opposite) A group of Confederate NCOs. Non-commissioned officers were vital to the functioning of a regiment. There would be a sergeant to every twenty enlisted men and a corporal to every ten. It was not uncommon for NCOs not to bother to wear their chevrons and those that were worn were sewn directly onto the jacket. The NCOs were the main fount of knowledge for drill and duties.

Flags and Drummers

FLAG uniformity was never achieved in the Confederate Army: the fiercely independent representatives of the different states jealously guarded their right to carry their silk and cotton state flags. Many of the flags had been adapted from local militia standards, and some units had flags that depicted the unit's nickname, such as Barlow's Yankee Killers. A wide variety of materials was used to produce the flags, including wedding dresses, grain sacks, and cotton, wool and silk. Many units would display their own unit flag, a state flag and the ubiquitous Stars and Bars. Eventually the Confederate Government did issue Stars and Bars and released regulations regarding banners, but to a large extent this was ignored by regiments determined to retain their state identity.

In order to reinforce the men's courage, Confederate musicians marched alongside the standards. Drummers would be used to help match the marching time of the regiment, while bugles, fifes and clarinets provided stirring and uplifting music to urge the men on. Many of the drummers were young boys, sons of the regiment or boys adopted as mascots by the men. Many of the young boys attached themselves to the regiments despite the fact they were not old enough to serve in the ranks.

(Below) A depiction of the 43rd North Carolina Volunteers. The first flag, predominantly blue, depicts the North Carolina state flag and is carried by a young recruit. The standard Stars and Bars is carried by a more senior man and the unit's regimental flag details the formation of the volunteer militia unit, which dates back to the American War of Independence. In this case the regiment was formed in May 1775. The re-muster as a Confederate regiment, according to the flag, took place in May 1861. This selection of standards is typical of Confederate regiments: pledging their allegiance to the Confederacy by carrying the Stars and Bars, while maintaining their identity as North Carolinians.

(Opposite) A Confederate drummer boy wearing a frock coat and typical style of forage cap worn by musicians during the American Civil War. He sits on a snare drum, which would have carrying straps. The drummer boy standing behind him wears a shorter coat with the oval Eastern Theatre Confederate buckle. The drummer boys would wear specially issued uniforms if they were lucky, but they were more likely to wear hastily adapted, and far larger, garments.

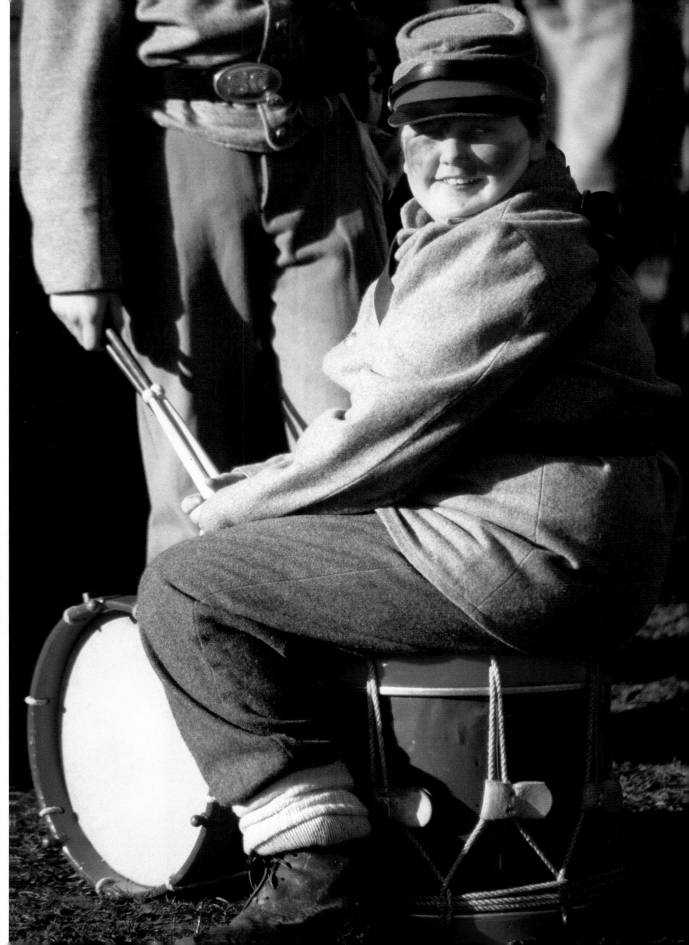

(Left) A variant of the Stars and Bars, this time cross-hatched rather than diagonal. The standard-bearer wears a long frock coat with a standard Confederate Eastern Theatre buckle plate around his waist. He is armed only with a pistol. The two privates wear typical Confederate uniform mixtures. The private on the left wears a butternut uniform with a stand-up collared jacket and broad-brimmed hat, while the private on the right wears light-blue trousers, a short, grey jacket and a kepi hat. Note the variations even in the grey of the uniforms.

(Below) Drummer boys leading the way for a large infantry column. The drummer in the second rank wears a militia waist belt with metal belt-plate. He has a Havelock over his kepi – this headgear was designed during the Indian Mutiny and used to protect the man's neck from sunshine. Several sets of Stars and Bars in different designs illustrate the variation of this standard banner. The drums were often painted with a mixture of Stars and Bars, state insignia and the regimental name or number.

(Below) A defiant standard-bearer placed at the centre of a Confederate skirmish line, fending off Union cavalry. The standard of a North Carolinian regiment depicts the Stars and Bars with the regiment's battle honours, in this case Harper's Ferry. Standard-bearers and officers tended not to adopt prone positions and as a consequence were often picked off by the enemy. The officer carries a cartridge box attached to a shoulder belt. This was a copy of the US Army pattern: inside he would have two tin containers, each carrying twenty cartridges.

(Right) While the majority of Stars and Bars were of the St Andrew's cross style, many units used this thirteen-starred battle flag. The standard-bearer wears a long frock coat, a civilian-style hat and predominantly black accoutrements, with a water bottle covered in grey material. The standard was used as a rallying point in fire-fights to mark the location of the regiment in the field; in advances and charges the standard would lead the way. Standard-bearers were often chosen men who had already displayed their valour on the battlefield. In attacks they would be expected to be in the leading elements of the regiment, ready to plant their flag on the captured enemy position. Like officers, standard-bearers suffered high casualties.

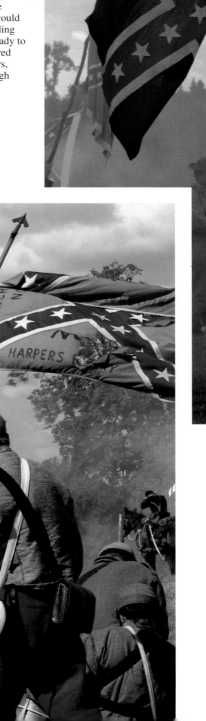

(Opposite) The full array of regimental musicians. The drums were vital in keeping the beat on the march, as well as for passing on orders in the field and in the camp. Various different drum slings were used. Note that two of the four drummers use the standard white cotton web drum sling. The musicians would lead the regiment until it had come into firing range, when they would be overtaken by the regiment, led by the officers. Musicians then adopted the role of medical orderlies, assisting the wounded, as well as bringing ammunition up to the firing line.

(Top left) An unadorned Confederate Government-issue St Andrew's cross-style Stars and Bars, with thirteen stars depicting the seceding states of the Confederacy. The standard is among a group of rank-and-file soldiers with a variety of different jackets and headgear. They each have black leather cap boxes with lamb's wool lining. Many would have the maker's name, or occasionally CS (Confederate States), stamped on them.

(Above) A selection of variants of the Stars and Bars, drawn from a number of different Confederate regiments from within the same division. In this case the majority of the standard-bearers are issued with Enfield rifled muskets. Again they have a wide range of different headgear and uniform variations. Some have government-issued grey trousers, while others have opted for captured Union blue.

(**Above**) This standard-bearer carries a southern-made cartridge box. It was a copy of the percussion rifle box that was introduced in 1850. Other men would have carried a copy of the US 1855 model, although there were still many who wore the M1842 box. There were several variations, but most could carry two tin containers. The standard-bearer also has a southern drum-style canteen -- many would have used imported British Army wooden canteens. This man's canteen has a leather strap and may be made of either cedar or cherry wood.

(**Opposite**) This standard-bearer wears the common stand-up-collar, unadorned jacket. His pistol holster, which appears to house a Colt Model 1848 army revolver, is visible. He wears a black, leather, southern-made cap box, approximately 2.5in deep and 1.25in thick (6.4 × 3.2cm) with lamb's wool lining.

(Left) This infantry standard-bearer wears a patched light-grey jacket with blue facings and CSA brass buttons. Under the jacket can be seen his waistcoat, which was not a part of regulation uniform. These jackets were made of lightweight wool or cotton and wool blend and usually had nine buttons and three or four slash pockets; some had standing collars. He wears a battered felt or leather hat, designed to keep the rain and sun out of his eyes.

(Opposite) A Texan unit advancing in line past deployed artillery. The Texan flag was another peculiarity of the south: while containing the ever-present red, white and blue, its predominant feature was a single 'lone star', an image associated with the state of Texas. The officers wear long frock coats with Austrian-knot detail on their cuffs. Both men wear civilian-style hats and are armed with cavalry sabres.

This Confederate standard-bearer carries a Spiller and Burr revolver for personal protection; this was a revolver favoured by many Confederates. His ragged appearance infers a later-war pattern of uniform, which would have been converted civilian clothing with military accoutrements and buttons added. He wears a civilian floppy hat for all-weather protection.

Infantry Enlisted Men

IN June 1861 the Confederate Government issued regulations that enlisted men were to be given a standard coat that resembled an officer's jacket. It was to lack the Austrian knots and only have two small buttons on each cuff. The collars and cuffs for standard infantry were to denote their branch of service. A year later, however, the majority of the men were wearing a jacket known as the 'roundabout'. This was a short-waisted, single-breasted jacket with a low-standing collar. Fewer than 20 per cent had frock coats, single- or double-breasted. Many of the men wore sack coats, rather like their officers. Men in the field adopted the simple expedient of acquiring their sack coats from the Union army; it would be standard procedure to bleach the jacket and then re-dye it grey. They would then add three buttons so that there would be seven buttons down the front. The men or the unit's camp followers often added a standing collar. The grey would run from a very dark shade, typical in the Army of Northern Virginia, to a brownish-grey. By 1864 brown became the most common colour; this was produced by dying the wool with a mixture of oils from the walnut tree and copperas, and gave rise to the famous butternut colour. A huge variety of different colours was produced, from a dusty white brown to the colour of coffee. Many of the jackets were homespun, simply adding to the wide variety of coloration.

A typical selection of uniforms, depicting the wide variety of grey and butternut uniforms regularly worn by the Confederate regiments. Not only are the jackets and trousers in a variety of colours, but they are also in a variety of different styles. Note also the different forms of kepi, civilian hat and captured Union headgear. The majority of the men seem to be armed with the Enfield musket. Equipment pouches vary from black to brown russet, which accurately reflects different periods of issue, as well as the use of captured equipment.

(Right) A typical group of late-war Confederate infantry about to leave on a foraging operation. The men wear their bedrolls strapped around their torsos and their other personal belongings are kept in haversacks. The figure in the foreground carries in addition to his bayonet a side knife, which would have been used for a variety of different purposes, both in camp and in the field.

(Below) Although 1861 regulations stated that Confederate infantry should wear sky-blue, cloth trousers, many of the officers and men had a fundamental problem with wearing blue. This was not just a political decision on behalf of the men: there had been innumerable cases when Confederates with even a part-blue uniform had been shot at by their own men. Major General Patrick Cleburne, in October 1863, reported that several of his men had been killed by their own artillery as a result of their wearing Union sky-blue trousers. This group has predominantly butternut and grey uniforms; a mixture of different cartridge and cap boxes is also visible, of varying pattern and colour.

(**Opposite**) Here a Confederate infantryman displays a more macabre use of his side knife. In many cases the opposing lines were literally within feet of one another. The fronts were always fluid and opportunities for infiltration and intelligence-gathering were a valuable adjunct to more conventional military intelligence. The Confederate is silencing his victim in order to maintain the secrecy of his presence so close to the enemy camp.

(**Below**) Pushing out a skirmish line in front of the regiment often allowed a numerically inferior Confederate force to be shielded and protected from a much larger Union unit. The Confederates were adept at using terrain and had a reputation for being good shots – many of the southern men were more accustomed to firearms than their northern opponents. In truth the best shots in a Confederate regiment were pushed forward, as they would waste less ammunition than the less-experienced men.

(**Right**) A skirmish line would be spread out in front of an advancing regiment. In theory the skirmishers were the principal target of the enemy. They had the advantage of being able to move more freely as they were not in dense formation. Skirmishers would be detached to deal with enemy skirmishes first, and then to engage the main enemy body. Officers and NCOs were prime targets.

(**Opposite**) Incoming fire from Confederate skirmishers often had the effect of demoralizing enemy regiments – on one occasion a Confederate officer accompanying a skirmish line accounted for twenty Union men. A group of skirmishers having approached the enemy, half of them would fire a volley, then reload while the remaining men engaged the enemy with their fire.

(**Above**) In areas where the Confederates were vastly outnumbered they could only hope to delay or draw away the enemy: snipers and sharpshooters could often delay or force back Union formations that were far larger than themselves. The effect of the sharpshooters was never conclusive on the battlefield, but on numerous occasions these unseen snipers would pick off officers on horseback or NCOs dressing the line.

(**Opposite top**) A kneeling or prone position was often adopted during a fire-fight, unless of course there was sufficient cover to protect a standing man. Loading while prone or kneeling was more complex, bearing in mind that the combined length of musket and ramrod was at least 8ft (2.4m). Aimed shots from behind picket fences tended to be more accurate, as the men could rest their weapons on the fence and concentrate on specific targets ahead of them.

(**Opposite left**) These infantrymen defending a picket fence appear to have removed the slings from their muskets. Slings were in short supply; they were made from cotton until 1864 and from reinforced leather thereafter. During the war the Richmond Arsenal managed to produce over 320,000 muskets, but less than half the number of slings required.

(**Above**) This Confederate regiment has adopted the prone position, facing the dual threat of Union Berdan Sharpshooters and mounted cavalry. The majority of the men have short shell jackets in a variety of greys and browns. The drummer boy still wears the official-issue frock coat. The infantry would instinctively seek what cover was available: instead of a regiment forming up according to drill training, they would hug the terrain and its features according to how the local farmer had arranged his ditches and fences, taking advantage of any slight contour in the land and refusing to budge from fence rails or standing crops.

(Above) A selection of predominantly grey- and brown-clad Confederate infantry. Most of the trousers were well worn, the majority of them patched and re-patched around the seat. Many opted for any form of cloth to patch their trousers, including material cut from enemy clothing and even blankets. Most of the trousers were made of wool, and in the Western Theatre the predominant form was grey jeans, though some opted for trousers made of blanket material. The majority of the trousers had a button fly, two front pockets, occasionally a watch pocket, and a belt or holes for lacing over a vent for size adjustment. The buttons were made of bone, metal or sometimes wood. The majority of the trousers had a small slit at the bottom of the leg seam.

(Opposite top) As the struggle continued towards its inevitable conclusion in 1865, most dress regulations were largely forgotten, as were recruitment policies. Increasingly regiments were filled with men who would previously have been excused duty because of age or infirmity, while young boys barely in their teens would take their place in the firing line. These men have a mixture of pre-war militia uniforms, captured US equipment and trousers, and homespun butternut clothing. Variations in kepi and forage cap can also be seen.

(Opposite below) A Confederate firing line, showing the men reloading their Enfield rifled muskets. It was late 1862 before the Confederacy was in a position to begin replacing obsolete flintlocks with percussion muskets. Even this was a gradual process, as local production was limited and overseas imports were difficult to acquire because of the Union blockade. The vast majority of the men were re-armed with captured US Army muskets: by September 1864 some 45,000 rifles had been captured during the year, compared with 30,000 that had been imported and just 20,000 produced in the Southern States.

(Opposite) There was an average of around 400 men in a Confederate regiment. They would open fire at around 150yd (140m) and halt some 50yd (45m) in front of the enemy. According to investigations made into fire-fights during the war, it would take in excess of 130 Confederate shots to hit a Union infantryman. The men were vulnerable when they were reloading their muskets: even a trained man would take at least 20–30 seconds to reload. During this time he would be standing in plain view of the enemy, with Minié bullets whistling around his ears.

(Above) Around 75 per cent of the imported muskets were English-made Enfields, or copies of the Enfield 1853 Model. Around one in five of the muskets were Austrian, based on the 1854 Rifled Musket – indeed, around 100,000 of these were imported. The remaining muskets came from a variety of sources including the German states, Belgium and France.

(Opposite top) Loading procedures were included in drill training, but in many cases the soldiers never got a chance to fire live ammunition before they were involved in a battle. The load sequence was complex: the soldier would have to hold the rifle away from the body, take the cartridge out of his pouch, tear the cartridge between his teeth, pour the powder into the muzzle followed by the bullet and paper, draw his rammer, ram the cartridge down the muzzle, return his rammer into its position alongside the musket barrel, prime his musket by placing the percussion cap on the nipple, shoulder the musket, and then make ready to fire by pointing it at a target and cocking the hammer before aiming and firing.

(Opposite below) According to the drills, each man was assumed to be able to fire three aimed rounds per minute; in reality it took a man between forty minutes and two hours to loose off forty rounds. The muskets would foul after a handful of shots and accuracy – not good even with the musket in clean condition – would be impaired even further. It was therefore likely that after an initial two or three volleys, one of the opposing regiments would either pull back or break. In the heat of battle fire control was virtually impossible due to the noise: officers could barely order their men to open fire and cease fire. Many of the men tended to shoot high, so they were often told to fire at the belt or the knees. Only the first shot could really be considered to be a volley, as after that the men would fire at will.

(Right) A Confederate corporal in a homespun, woollen butternut jacket and matching kepi cap. Officially, according to Confederate War Department regulations, the standard headgear for the Confederate infantry was the kepi. No colour was stated, but it was suggested that there should be some blue coloration to denote that the hat was worn by an infantryman. Enlisted men were supposed to wear their regimental number on the cap front. Many of the peaks were made of cardboard and covered in black-painted cloth. Many of the men made their own hats out of woollen shirts and leather. The wide variety of headgear worn by the infantry is testament to the fact that no kepis or hats were distributed in large numbers after the first few months of the war.

(Right) By February 1863 the London Armoury had exported over 70,000 rifled muskets to the Southern States. After this period they were, on average, shipping 1,300 rifled muskets to the Confederacy each month. When the Confederates captured the rifle machinery from Harper's Ferry armoury this was shipped to Richmond, where nearly 12,000 copies of the US Springfield were made.

(Opposite) Many of the muskets dated back to the Napoleonic era and had been improved only by the addition of a percussion-cap priming system instead of flintlock priming. In the early years smooth-bore muskets outnumbered rifled muskets by four to one. Confederate troops went into battle armed with a huge variety of different weapons, including their own shotguns and squirrel guns. By 1863, 30 per cent of the Confederate infantry was still armed with smooth bores. These Enfield rifled muskets have fixed bayonets. The use of the bayonet was a last-ditch option if the unit was about to be overrun or had run out of ammunition – according to records in 1864 only fifty US casualties of the 50,000 killed or wounded that year fell to the bayonet.

(Right) Although kepis were the intended standard headgear, they were not the preferred hats of the soldiers. A wide variety of slouch hats, palmettos, straw hats and even quilted cloth hats was worn. The kepi offered no protection from the sun or rain, so all kinds of styles, shapes and brands were adopted at the men's personal preference. This man wears a civilian shirt. Although all enlisted men were supposed to have three flannel shirts issued each year, either in red or white, the reality of the situation was that shirts from home were the most popular.

(Opposite) This infantryman wears the standard six-piece body, two-piece sleeve and five-buttoned shell jacket. His only insignia is a badge on his kepi and a plate on one of his straps.

(Above) This infantryman wears a wool-weft, cotton-warp, jean-weave material jacket in a grey/brown colour. It appears to be a standard-patterned shell jacket, with no trim. Under his jacket he has a striped, collarless civilian shirt. His kepi, made of similar material to his jacket, has more of a grey hue with a stiff, black leather peak and what appear to be state brass buttons.

(Right) An infantryman, standing alongside other members of his unit. His issue cotton haversack has had its strap knotted so that it fits snugly to his hip. His cartridge strap appears to be of thin cotton material. Note the loops around the waist of his jacket, which are designed to prevent his belt and cap box from slipping out of reach.

(**Left**) This is a private of the 43rd North Carolina Infantry. He belongs to Company B, as can be seen by the brass letter on his kepi. His jacket is predominantly made of grey wool, with no adornments apart from the brass buttons.

(**Opposite top**) This infantry private has opted for a civilian high-crown, broad-brimmed hat with a narrow silk headband. He wears round spectacles typical of the period. Note his bayonet, which has ridges in order to plunge more easily into bodies and to be withdrawn with the minimum of force.

(**Opposite below left**) A Confederate infantryman wearing a slouch hat. He, too, has opted for a civilian shirt, the most popular being checks, stripes and calico, although some infantrymen wore plaid or polka-dot shirts. In practice barely a quarter of the men would have worn kepis; the rest would have worn slouch hats, predominantly tan, grey, black or dark brown in colour. This infantryman's hat has a brim of up to 4in (10cm) and a black silk ribbon around the band. It has a crown of approximately 4.5in (11.5cm).

(**Opposite below right**) An alternative kepi style, this time with a grey/green crown and brass lettering. The peak appears to be stiff black leather, fixed to a black cotton jean-like material. He wears a rough, light-grey jacket patched in blue with light-blue facings. Under his jacket are his clearly visible long johns. Standard-issue undergarments rarely fitted the men and, as can be seen from this example, the private has opted for a captured Union undergarment.

(**Left**) Infantry carried a variety of different canteens. Here the central figure is holding a southern-style tin-drum canteen. His companion has a captured smooth-sided Federal-pattern canteen. Others would include Gardner cedar-wood drum-style, or other patterns.

(**Below**) This infantry corporal has opted for a light-brown slouch hat with a tan band. His companions wear other varieties, including a black, broad-brimmed hat and a tan, domed civilian hat. The men are predominantly wearing light grey with black accoutrements. They carry their personal belongings and bedrolls, a common feature of Confederate troops on campaign.

(**Below**) A selection of typical Confederate equipment. Most bayonets were carried in a brown or black leather scabbard, often with a brass tip. The bayonet usually had an 18in (46cm) blade and a 3in (7.5cm) socket. The standard Confederate cap pouch is clearly visible. Many of these were either produced by southern arsenals or imported from Britain. Many of the men actually preferred to carry their caps in either their jacket or waistcoat pockets, as the cap pouches were fastened with either a central fastening strap or fastening studs, which were tricky to undo in the heat of battle.

(**Above**) Typical infantry equipment, consisting of a bayonet in a leather sheath, a cartridge box, a cap box and a southern-made, drum-style tin canteen. In practice, many of the Confederates preferred the US Army canteen: a new recruit could easily be spotted in a Confederate regiment as he would still be carrying his standard-issue canteen, while most of the other men would have discarded theirs in preference to a US one. The shoulder belt of the canteen is in white cotton, while the other equipment has leather shoulder belts. In practice, leather was replaced with several layers of cotton stitched together and then painted black. Confederates were not issued with shoulder straps for their cartridge belts, so they either made their own or used captured equipment.

(Left) Bayonets only tended to be fixed for sentry duty or for an extreme situation on the battlefield. On the battlefield men would avoid fixing bayonets, as they interfered with loading and shooting. They were also reluctant to fix bayonets as it meant they would have to jettison their personal equipment in order to take a charge. Strangely, though, bayonet drills were far more common than target practice. In practice, the men would be more likely to use their muskets as clubs than to attempt to skewer their enemy with the bayonet.

(Opposite) Close combat was relatively rare. Fire-fights could last for several hours either side of a defensive position. In hand-to-hand combat muskets could be used either conventionally with their bayonets for fencing, or as a club. Bayonets were used as candlesticks in camp and as skewers on a cooking fire; many men would bend them to create hooks for hanging pots over fires. They were also used to loosen earth when digging trenches.

(**Opposite**) Confederate infantry habitually wore their blanket rolls across their shoulders, usually tied together with string and slung loosely over their equipment. They would have a variety of different blankets, only a handful being official army issue. Many used captured US Army blankets, while others preferred the comfort of a blanket from home. On average they were around 5ft (1.5m) square, made of wool, and they could be of literally any colour.

These men are all clothed in later-period butternut uniforms. The men in the foreground have already loaded and primed their muskets and are ready to deliver a volley. The Enfield .577 rifle musket had a slightly better performance than the .58 Springfield M1861.

(Left) This infantry officer has an elaborate selection of different straps to carry his equipment. His waterproof, leather haversack contains his blanket roll and is attached to two stout shoulder straps. His sword is slung over his right shoulder, as is his haversack. He wears a double-breasted grey jacket with a single star, denoting that he is a second lieutenant.

(Above) Here a Confederate infantryman displays a brown leather cartridge box with the oval CS brass plate. He appears to have a civilian all-purpose knife and a black southern-made leather cap box. His tunic, denoting the rank of sergeant, is patched at the elbow by a plaid material from a civilian shirt. He carries a white haversack, probably made of cotton. Many Confederate infantry carried captured US Army haversacks, while others used copies of British-made models. Most of the haversacks were limp and probably converted or amended in some way to suit the individual's preferences.

(Opposite) Another view of the sergeant, this time accompanied by a private with a dark-grey blanket and a black leather cartridge pouch. The private's water bottle has a white cotton strap with a leather casing and cork stopper. All of the men in the group wear variations of the slouch hat or civilian broad-brimmed hat. The corporal has an additional rolled groundsheet.

(Right) An archetypal Confederate infantryman, with his short, rough, homespun jacket and butternut-style trousers. He carries a haversack. Originally these haversacks were to be white cotton with the regimental number, name and company letter, along with the soldier's number, marked in black on the flap. In practice, however, as can be seen in this picture, the infantryman has opted for a captured US-issue waterproof haversack. According to some accounts, by the spring of 1862 very few infantrymen in the Army of Northern Virginia were carrying anything but captured US Army haversacks.

(Below) This picture suggests that many of the men opted to sling their blanket rolls across their right shoulder in order to reduce the effect of the recoil of the musket. Firing for prolonged periods of time not only produced large volumes of smoke, but it could also cause injuries to the soldiers' shoulders and firing arms. Here the men are forming up in support of a Confederate artillery unit. They wear a variety of grey and butternut, and an assortment of hats and kepis.

(Opposite top) Theoretically, each man was to be issued with four pairs of socks a year. In reality this was never achieved, nor would this small issue ever have been sufficient. Many of the men wrapped their feet in rags and their shoes would have been full of holes. The availability of boots and shoes was also limited. The men wore a boot known as the Jefferson, which was ankle high with two or three pairs of holes for the laces. Officially they were supposed to be black with square toes, although many were produced in various shades of brown.

(Opposite below) One of the men in the foreground wears gaiters. They were not official issue and were actually made for the quartermaster's corps, but some regiments managed to obtain them early in the war. They were made of white cotton and had a leather strap that passed underneath the boot. The gaiters reached halfway up to the knee and covered the top of the boot. In this example the infantryman has four leather straps and buckles, although many were fastened with a row of bone or wooden buttons.

(Above) With the exception of his trousers, this infantryman wears standard regulation cadet grey. His shouldered musket, once the bayonet had been fitted, would give him a reach of approximately 8ft (2.4m). The infantryman has a striped, cotton haversack with a single bone button. His metal cup is probably standard issue and he has a wooden canteen reinforced with leather straps and rivets.

(Right) This picture depicts a Confederate corporal in the process of reaching for a cartridge out of his cartridge belt. Veteran men such as these sought to lead by example. The men around him are prone and his battlefield role was to be ever present for signs of the men breaking, and to direct the men to deal with threats as they presented themselves.

(**Above**) Despite the lack of adequate issues of clothing and equipment, Confederate regiments were blessed with an intense *esprit de corps*, which transcended the privations that they faced in the field. There were inevitably some stragglers as by late 1862, due to boot shortages, many of the men were barefooted. Some were ordered to make their own moccasins from slaughtered cattle hide. Some shoes had leather or canvas uppers and wooden soles. US Army shoes and boots were the most popular because generally they were of far higher quality.

(Below) Before moving off toward the battlefield, a regiment would take advantage of the last few minutes to check their equipment, finish a cigar or replenish their canteens. This group of North Carolina Infantry, in a variety of standard and non-standard clothing and headgear, have variously opted to attach their bayonets or to leave them in their scabbards. The drummer wears what appears to be a captured Union musician's overcoat with extensive braiding to the front and cuffs.

(Opposite top) On campaign the infantrymen's uniform and equipment would be put to the most rigorous of tests. Many of the boots were imported directly from Britain. They were lined and filled with stiff paper, which meant that if the soldier had to cross a river or was in rainy conditions the boots quickly began to fall apart. The boots were made of half-cured green leather and after just a week the heel would have gone and the sole would be virtually non-existent.

(Opposite below) A Confederate North Carolina Infantry company on the move. A non-commissioned officer lacking any distinguishing insignia commands the unit. A corporal leads the front rank following the drummer; a single star remnant of a flag is fixed to his bayonet. Note the sword-like bayonet on the rifle of the man on the right in the leading line, next to the corporal. All of the men retain vestiges of their original issue uniform, apart from a private in the third rank from the rear, who appears to be wearing a homespun checked hunting shirt.

(Right) When the regiment finally arrived on the battlefield it would form its companies in lines, two deep. The two flanking companies would be pushed forward as skirmishers and the regiment's standard would be placed behind the fifth company, defended by a party of nine non-commissioned officers. (The number of companies in a regiment varied from as few as five to a maximum of ten.) To the rear were the regimental officers, musicians, medical orderlies, the regiment's chaplain and other non-combatants.

(**Left**) By mid-1863 the grey, waist-length jacket was almost universal among Confederate infantry. It was at this point that any conformity of colour or style ended. The jackets varied tremendously in terms of composition and quality. Wool was desirable at least in poor weather conditions, but the men would have favoured cotton in warmer weather. Here we see an infantry regiment advancing with the widest possible variety of grey uniforms. Headgear in this regiment ranges from standard grey kepis and broad-brimmed, civilian-style hats to captured Union kepis and Hardee hats.

(**Above**) Depot-manufactured clothing continued to be in short supply despite the fact that the south was at the heart of the agriculture, notably the cotton industry, of the United States. The north had supplemented its blockade of the southern ports by laying waste the southern countryside and destroying stocks of cotton and wool. In late 1863 a representative of the British Army offered to supply 50,000 sets of jackets and matching trousers to the Confederate Army before the end of the spring of 1864. The garments were manufactured in Ireland and were made of the finest cadet-grey cloth. Only troops based in Virginia and North Carolina benefited from this new issue.

(Opposite) This standard-pattern butternut jacket, a homespun mix of wool, cotton and jean material, has an unadorned stand-up collar and simple brass buttons. The private has a civilian-style slouch hat with a high crown and silk headband. He is carrying his musket in the sloped-arms position, which was the most comfortable means of carrying it. His left hand supports the rifle butt. He would normally carry around forty rounds of ammunition, but if moving through enemy territory or facing an immediate attack, the infantryman would be given anything up to an additional sixty rounds. He would have several days' worth of food in his haversack and would be carrying other essential items such as kettle, frying pan, private papers, drinking cup and perhaps a book.

(Right) This group of Confederate infantry's clothing is in stark contrast to the intended grey of the Confederate Army. The majority wear a mixture of coats, blouses and jackets, dyed in a mixture of colours from tan to brown. The majority of the jackets are made from jean-like material. Confederate infantry were not issued with summer-weight trousers; their trousers were often made from the same cotton/wool jean cloth that was used for the jackets, while others were made entirely from cotton. The campaigns took a heavy toll on uniforms, particularly trousers. Typically, Confederate infantry are seen wearing ragged trousers: such was the nature of the continued marching and manoeuvring that even the heavy wool Union trousers wore out quickly. It is therefore not surprising that the Confederates adopted any type of trousers available and were keen to retain even the most patched garment.

(Left) A member of B Company of the 43rd North Carolina regiment enjoys a cigar before moving toward the battlefield. A regiment moved along a road in columns of three or four, with a yard between each man; a full-strength regiment would then occupy 250yd (230m) of road. For the most part, however, by the time baggage, camp followers and cattle were taken into account, a regiment would occupy at least 500yd (460m) of road. The men travelled light, jettisoning everything that was not immediately needed. They faced a routine of marching, foraging and then finding an appropriate, hopefully sheltered, place to camp for the night. It was not unusual for a man to carry as much as 40–60lb (18–27kg) of equipment.

(Above) After the first few volleys had been fired on the battlefield the infantrymen would have a very restricted field of vision. Their senses would be dominated by the musketry fire and shouted instructions from their officers and non-commissioned officers. Here we see an infantry regiment in a firing line, supported by a second regiment moving up. The standard, being the symbol of the regiment's fighting spirit, is held aloft and used as the identification of a rallying point should the regiment break. A rough estimate of the enemy's strength could be gauged by counting the number of standards. Like officers', standard-bearers' life expectancy was short and in hard-fought battles several men would successively hold the banner aloft after their fellow southerner had been hit or killed.

(Left) This veteran infantryman would have been typical of the men who survived three or more years of continued movement throughout the war. They were experts at acquiring fresh vegetables, meat and even shoe leather along the route of marching. The men would rise early and begin with a breakfast

(Opposite) Men of a regiment held in reserve with sloped muskets. The picture illustrates three common forms of infantry jacket and trousers, ranging from the early issue grey with blue facing, including that on the kepi, to either state or homespun stand-up collar jackets in various shades of butternut. The men have a mixture of headgear, including a butternut kepi, a stiff, tan broad-brimmed hat with a white silk headband and a more formal black, probably felt, civilian hat.

at dawn. They would march two-thirds of their intended distance and then stop for a lunch. After this they would forage and then camp. A usual marching day, including rest periods, was eight hours, and in good conditions they would be able to cover around 2½ miles (4km) per hour.

(**Opposite top**) The infantry would open fire around 100yd (90m) from the enemy, a single regiment of around 400 men using about 3.5lb (1.6kg) of powder per volley. Battles were noisy and could be heard up to 60 miles (100km) away. Once the men had started firing it was difficult to order them to stop until their ammunition had been used up. The men are standing shoulder-to-shoulder. Many would be anxious not to appear cowardly in front of their peers. The crucial time came after the first few shots, as this was when casualties could cause panic to spread through the regiment and once one group had chosen to flee the rest of the regiment would surely follow. A whole Confederate brigade fled at the battle of Antietam (17 September 1862).

(**Opposite below**) In the heat of battle many of the men would forget or ignore standard loading-drill training; pictured here is a prime example of a group of Confederate infantrymen at various stages of the reloading process. The infantryman in the centre has only just retrieved his cartridge from his pouch. The man on the right has already bitten the cartridge and is in the process of dropping its contents into the barrel of the musket. The heavily accoutred infantryman on the left has already completed his loading sequence and is pulling back the hammer on his musket. In the densely packed ranks the men often obstructed one another, making the loading drill difficult. The men in the rear ranks had to make sure that they did not shoot their own men in front of them. Psychologically the men would group closely together, but for practical purposes it was better to have some space between each of the men.

(**Above**) A view from the rear of a Confederate firing line. Note the preponderance of shell jackets in various colours and the single frock coat of the private second from the left. The regiment has delivered a volley and is beginning to reload. Note that as the unit is stationary the majority of the men have not refastened the catches on their cartridge pouches. The men wear a mixture of shoes and boots, some with knitted socks, while others wear captured US Army socks. The socks were usually white and made from cotton or a cotton and wool mix. The trouser legs were invariably tucked into them. The men wore the socks as replacements for gaiters, and would usually tie them in place with string.

Cavalry

AT the outbreak of the American Civil War the US Army had five regiments of cavalry. There were two dragoon regiments, one mounted rifle regiment and two conventional cavalry regiments; they had been operating almost exclusively along the Western Frontier against Native Americans.

To begin with the Confederate Army had very few cavalry – when the Civil War broke out in 1861 the majority of the enlisted cavalrymen were loyal to the Union, but several of the officers had Confederate sympathies. Among the cavalry commanders who defected to the Confederacy were Robert E. Lee, Albert Sidney Johnston, William Hardee, J.E.B. Stuart, John Bell Hood, Richard Ewell, Earl Van Dorn and Joseph Wheeler. In the early years Confederate cavalry were not only more proficient but in higher numbers than the Union and J.E.B. Stuart's black horse cavalry terrified Union infantrymen.

Men believed that glory could be found in the saddle rather than in the ranks of the infantry. Individual colonels would be given authority to raise new regiments and consequently uniforms widely differed, as did equipment and weapons. Particularly feared were the Confederate Mounted Raiders, armed with a variety of weapons including sabres and shotguns.

Unless the infantry was caught unprepared, as was often the case, the cavalry could not deliver the knockout blow that their predecessors had achieved during the Napoleonic Wars. Cavalry were ideal scouts, suited to taking ground, but only capable of holding it for a limited period of time without infantry and artillery support.

Theoretically, cavalry uniforms did not differ greatly from those of the infantry, with the major distinction of having a bright yellow trim instead of a blue infantry trim.

(**Below**) A Confederate cavalry officer wearing a southern-style broad-brimmed hat, an army-issue undershirt and light-blue trousers with a yellow stripe. The officer has a pistol for a sidearm, but is primarily armed with a carbine. The officer may be carrying a British Terry's pattern 1860 carbine with a breech mechanism or a Keen, Walker & Co. breech-loading carbine. He carries a bedroll attached to the rear of his saddle, but otherwise all of his personal effects and other equipment are hanging from the two black leather shoulder straps.

(**Opposite top**) These Confederate infantrymen are about to surge forward to take a position. Officers encouraged shouting and yelling and the 'Rebel Yell' was designed to induce panic amongst the Union ranks. Regiments from different states had their own oaths and yells, and these were used to keep up the momentum of charging troops. These men have not yet fixed bayonets.

(**Opposite**) In the heat of battle prisoners faced a high risk of being shot by a frenzied enemy; otherwise, they were usually treated reasonably well. Here two Confederate prisoners are ushered into camp by members of a Union brigade. Scattered regiments were difficult to reform, but many men would rally at a designated point in the hope that they could meet up with their unit. Prisoners would be sent to the rear and fed if there were sufficient supplies, but they would be shot if they attempted to escape. Exchanges of prisoners were common in the early years of the war, but by 1864 the Union had refused to continue this practice as it allowed the south to replace its combat losses. Thousands died in prison camps in both the north and the south.

(Above) The same cavalry officer is shown here ahead of his troop, skirmishing with Union infantry. The officer can be seen carrying what appears to be a Model 1840 cavalry sabre in its scabbard. He is sitting in a Model 1859 McClellan saddle. Many officers preferred short roundabout jackets to their regulation frock coats, and cavalry officers did not tend to wear the Austrian knot on their cuffs. Initially they would have used an official dark-grey saddle blanket with a 3in (7.5cm) red border, with the letters 'CS' in orange at the centre of the blanket. In practice, however, virtually any type of blanket was used, as can be seen in this picture.

(Left) This Confederate cavalry guidon bearer has an 1859-pattern McClellan saddle, which had the advantage of being simpler and less expensive than existing saddles. It was light enough not to burden the horse, while at the same time was strong enough to support the rider and his equipment. The stirrups had a thick leather skirt that protected the cavalryman's boots from rocks and brush. The seat was covered with rawhide instead of leather, making it uncomfortable for the rider if it split. Due to the lack of leather in the south many of the

(Opposite) This cavalry officer is fortunate to have been issued with cavalry boots. The vast majority of the enlisted men would have been issued with shoes at a rate of at least eight to one, compared with the issue of boots. Given the shortage of leather for the making of boots in the south, it was imperative to protect this valuable footwear, even though for the majority of time the men would have been in the saddle. This officer has an early regulation saddlecloth of grey with yellow trim. His short forage jacket has broad yellow trim and an Austrian-knot design on the sleeve and cuff.

McClellan saddles had skirts of painted canvas instead of leather. Many Confederates used their own horses and civilian saddles. The smaller swallow-tail-shape cavalry standard was far more practical to carry on horseback than the standard infantry flag; normally the guidon was a state flag, or a variant on the Stars and Bars banner.

(**Opposite top**) The standard Confederate cavalry jacket had nine buttons and the only major difference from a standard uniform jacket was the yellow trim. The majority of the cavalry jackets had brass buttons with the letter 'C', standing for cavalry, stamped onto them. Many of the men were only issued with a standard jacket and did not have the option of a fatigue jacket and a dress jacket. It was therefore common for the men to reserve their jacket for parades and important occasions, and to wear a simple shirt in the field.

(**Opposite below**) In addition to ensuring that his own equipment was kept in serviceable order, the cavalryman was also responsible for ensuring that his horse and its equipment were regularly maintained. The picture depicts a typical bridle and bit arrangement for Confederate cavalry during the Civil War. Horses needed to be responsive to their rider, who would often have to manoeuvre his mount while loading and firing a carbine, often in difficult terrain. In the majority of cases a cavalry unit would deploy up to two-thirds of its strength as skirmishers, effectively mounted infantry. A section would be retained as horse holders and to prevent the mounts from bolting when the firing began.

(**Above**) In theory each Confederate cavalry regiment consisted of five squadrons, each with two companies of around eighty men. Cavalry usually operated in columns in order to manoeuvre over difficult terrain. It was rare to see a Confederate cavalry regiment deployed in line. Cavalrymen believed themselves to be members of an elite force and they were desperate to retain their yellow facings. Initially uniform regulations called for a grey forage cap with a yellow band around the lower edge. This was amended in early 1862, stating that the cap itself should be yellow and that there should be a dark blue band. In practice, cavalry units received either caps or hats, and only the Army of Northern Virginia seems to have ever received regular issues.

(Above) Confederate cavalry, like their infantry counterparts, obtained their headgear and uniforms from a wide variety of sources. Although caps were easier to produce, many of the men opted to discard the caps and wear broader-brimmed hats, which were capable of keeping out the worst of the weather. This mixed group of Confederate cavalry, commanded by a corporal, has both the McClellan skirted stirrup and also the civilian-style open stirrup. They are all wearing cavalry boots.

(Left) Long hair and slouch hats were typical of Confederate cavalry. The officer – who appears to be a lieutenant – wears a short, washed-out grey jacket with regulation yellow collar and cuffs. The Confederates nicknamed the Austrian-knot design 'chicken guts'. His high boots were popular and often they had a high flap to protect the knee. Many of the enlisted men, if not the officers, abandoned their sabres early on in the war, preferring to concentrate on the use of their carbines and pistols.

(Opposite) This man wears what appears to be an infantryman's shell jacket, with seven buttons. He is wearing a pair of civilian trousers and a broad-brimmed hat fastened to his head with a chinstrap. Around the band is black, knotted braid. Similar clothing would have been worn by the men under the command of Nathan Bedford Forrest, a hard-fighting but notorious Confederate cavalry officer who was later deeply involved in the creation of the Klu Klux Klan. Men from the 1st Virginia Cavalry Regiment in the first two years of the war wore a distinctive all-grey uniform with black trim, reminiscent of a dragoon's uniform. They wore black, broad-brimmed hats with plumes and even in the later stages of the war they attempted to retain their black facings.

(**Above**) This man wears a faded grey shell jacket with turned-up collar and light-blue regulation trousers. A chinstrap holds on his broad-brimmed hat, which has a yellow cord tied in a knot on the front of the crown to denote his branch of the service. His single breasted jacket has the standard seven buttons. His belt has what appears to be a Virginia state seal belt-plate next to his percussion-cap pouch, with a single strap held in place with a punched-through rivet.

(**Opposite top**) The leading figure in this photograph appears to be an officer lacking any indication of his rank. He carries a Model 1860 cavalry sabre, safely housed in a protective scabbard that is also made of metal. The hand-guard had several different variations, but was usually three-barred. Under his plain grey patrol jacket he wears a waistcoat. He has equipment attached to both the front and the rear of the saddle. He has a broad, white cotton haversack strap across his chest and further straps over his left shoulder for his cartridge belt and his cap box. He appears to be escorting a captured Union officer.

(**Opposite below**) This Confederate cavalry bugler appears to be wearing standard grey shell jacket and trousers with yellow trim. He has a broad-brimmed hat with a yellow cord and chinstrap. He would have been primarily, if not solely, armed with a Remington New Army Revolver in a holster. His cartridge belt can be seen on his back, attached to a belt. Buglers were used to sound formation changes, charges, recalls and other signals in battle. They would also be used as dispatch riders, as a means of contact between the regiment and the divisional commanders.

(Below) This large cavalry unit accurately illustrates the wide variety of military and civilian clothing and headgear worn by a typical Confederate regiment. The majority of the men would be armed with a Model 1859 Sharp's carbine. The purpose of cavalry during the Civil War was to find the enemy's weaknesses and clear avenues of approach for the infantry. They were also used as manoeuvring and blocking forces, able to ride to a position, dismount and hold the position before remounting and manoeuvring around the enemy's flank or rear. Armed with carbines, a cavalry skirmish line could be effective and would have been perfectly capable of holding back massed infantry for at least a short period of time.

(Opposite left) This advance party of cavalry scouts is assessing the lie of the land in advance of the main force. Both armies relied on cavalry to be their eyes and ears. Feints, probes and all-out attacks could be launched on prepared or unprepared positions. The Confederates used their cavalry in a semi-strategic sense, using them to spearhead the Army. All success depended upon surprise and speed and, above all, knowing where the enemy was before he knew your position. These men are dressed predominantly in grey and have a mixture of short riding boots, long boots to the knee and standard-issue shoes. They wear a variety of different headgear, including a broad-brimmed black hat with yellow braid and feather plume. The cavalryman to the far right wears gauntlets, favoured when the cavalry were to use their sabres in close combat.

(Right) If the cavalryman was fortunate he would be issued with an overcoat or a poncho. According to regulations this would be of grey wool and cut in exactly the same way as the Federal cavalryman's issue clothing. Confederates prized those manufactured in Britain but increasingly, as the war continued and the naval blockade strengthened its grip around the Confederacy, these were harder to come by. Although the figure depicted wears a grey poncho and overcoat, one of around 50,000 that arrived from Britain over the winter months of 1863–4, many of the cavalry risked wearing captured blue Union overcoats. The cavalryman carries a Model 1840 cavalry sabre with brass hand-guard, secured in a iron and steel scabbard.

(Left) A dismounted Confederate irregular cavalryman. Many *ad hoc* raiding parties and guerrilla groups were formed, particularly toward the end of the war. Jessie James had been a member of William Quantrill's Partisan Raiders. The men wore a wide variety of military and civilian clothing, often with feathers or bunches of ribbons in their hats. Quantrill's men were involved in numerous raids, often targeting civilians or African Americans. They would cheerfully kill or burn anyone and anything. Towards the end of the war Quantrill fled towards Texas and his guerrilla band split up. He was eventually killed on a raid in Kentucky in 1865. Frank and Jessie James and Cole and Jim Younger, who had all served with Quantrill, used their ex-commander's raiding tactics as an integral part of their bank and train robberies.

(Below) As the war drew to a close the Confederates became increasingly desperate due to their inability to hold positions and prevent Union troops from occupying much of the south. Their irregular cavalry units targeted supply dumps and any type of government property, as well as the civilian population. In many respects the cavalry, now virtually civilian uniformed, with only a semblance of military costume, were little more than mounted bandits, equipped with captured enemy equipment, civilian gear and whatever remained of any official issues of clothing or equipment from the past.

This colour party group depicts
both the Washington Artillery
and the 1st Rockbridge Artillery.
The latter operated initially in the
Shenandoah Valley under
Stonewall Jackson, having been
created on 12 May 1861. They
were present at Chancellorsville
and bombarded the Union lines
on Culp's Hill at Gettysburg; in
1864 they were instrumental in
stopping the Union advances at
Spotsylvania and Cold Harbor.
They were active during the
defence of Richmond. The unit
made a heroic stand at
Cumberland Church during Lee's
retreat to Appomattox Court
House and finally surrendered
under Captain Graham on 9 April
1865. Over the period of four
years over 400 men served in the
Rockbridge Artillery and the unit
took part in thirty-two battles.
The Washington Artillery is
depicted as carrying a Louisiana
state flag on a red field, while the
Rockbridge Artillery has a
regimental version of the Stars
and Bars.

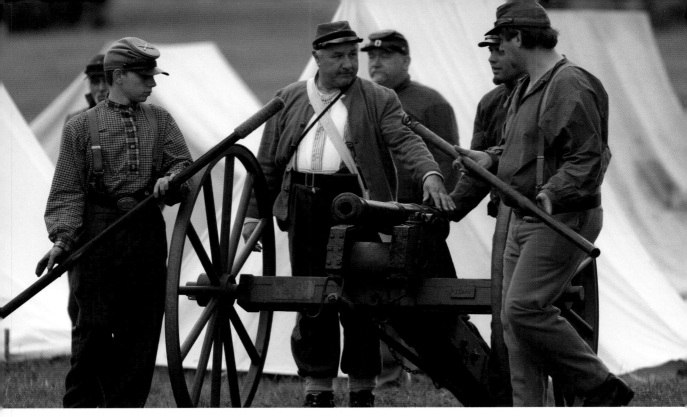

(Above) Like their infantry counterparts, many of the artillery enlisted men wore different forms of headgear. Here we see two variations of the standard kepi: one is almost identical to the infantry kepi, with the exception of the band around the crown, which is red instead of blue. The central figure providing instruction wears a predominantly red kepi with a black band and leather peak. The majority of the men wore army-issue shoes or boots, which were identical in quality and durability to those worn by the infantry. The men depicted here wear a variety of different-coloured trousers, held up by braces either over civilian shirts or undergarments. The artillery piece depicts the most common Confederate ordnance, a bronze, smooth-bore 12lb 'Napoleon' gun howitzer.

(Opposite below) An artillery officer, a sergeant and enlisted men take their place in an infantry column. The standard jacket and trouser issue was the same as for the infantry except that for the artillery they were trimmed with the distinctive red or scarlet. The men wearing dress coats are wearing coats identical to those issued to infantrymen. In practice the vast majority wore a fatigue blouse that was often worn by other infantry enlisted men. The stripe down the leg of the artillery sergeant was also common, and in the majority of cases the uniform was of a standard grey, as worn by the man in front of the sergeant. With the exception of distinctive units, such as the Washington Artillery, there was generally no distinction between heavy and light artillery units; it was merely the red trim that distinguished an artilleryman.

Artillery

THE artillery was seen as a supporting arm for the cavalry and the infantry in the Confederate Army. Artillery alone could not win a battle, let alone the war. The artillery was the smallest branch of the army, although the Confederacy mustered 268 batteries, battalions and regiments by the end of the war, amounting to 18 per cent of their total force. In comparison the Union enlisted 432 batteries, but these accounted for just 12 per cent of all units.

For centuries before the American Civil War artillery had been designated as either light or heavy. In simple terms, light guns were deployed on the battlefield while heavy guns were used against fortifications. Unlike locally raised and equipped regiments, the artillery had to rely on the Confederate Government to equip them.

At the beginning of the American Civil War a battery was attached to each brigade of infantry. Eventually batteries were grouped into battalions and operated independently from the infantry. The majority of the batteries had three, but more commonly two, sections and each section had two guns. Twenty-five men were assigned to each gun, nine of whom directly served the gun on the battlefield. In practice, however, each gun was likely to have as few as fifteen men who would man the gun and limber, prepare the shot and protect the horses. A battery consisting of four guns, up to ninety men and a similar number of horses would take up a considerable amount of space on the battlefield. The standard Confederate 'Napoleon' artillery piece (so called because it was based on a Napoleonic-era design) supposedly had around 230 rounds per gun, carried by the battery and consisting mainly of shells and solid shot, though on campaign a Confederate gun crew would be lucky indeed to have 230 rounds to last them for the duration of the battle.

(Right) The artillery officer wears a close approximation of regulation dress. His jacket is trimmed with red facing, denoting the artillery branch. He has two gold bars on his collar, signifying his rank as a lieutenant. On his red-topped kepi he has a distinctive brass, crossed artillery barrel insignia. The two men depict the Washington Artillery, which hailed from New Orleans. Traditionally they had worn dark-blue frock coats trimmed with red. These two men now wear Confederate grey, but retain their original kepis. This unit was part of the Army of Northern Virginia, and initially consisted of a battalion of four companies, but a fifth company was formed in New Orleans in February 1862. It did not serve with the rest of the battalion in Virginia and saw its first action with the Army of Tennessee at the battle of Shiloh in April 1862.

(Above) A Confederate artillery gun crew in the process of loading their 'Napoleon' 12-pounder. It was capable of firing solid shot, which was ideal for targets up to 1,600yd (1,500m) away. It could also fire spherical case or shrapnel that could be fuzed so that it would burst in the air above the enemy; this shot had an effective range of 800yd (750m). Filling the gap between the shrapnel and the round shot was the common shell – a hollow sphere filled with powder, with a time-fuze designed to burst on the ground when the enemy approached. At close range the artillery piece could deliver grapeshot, case or canister: these were tins full of round balls or shards of metal, making the gun in effect a huge shotgun and an extremely effective anti-infantry weapon.

(Opposite top) Commanders would place artillery batteries to cover vulnerable parts of their front, in the hope that they would dissuade enemy units from approaching. Artillery could also be used offensively to 'soften up' the enemy. In many cases, 10 per cent casualties could convince even the most determined units to pull back out of range. In some battles the artillery wreaked enormous damage: at Fredericksburg around 20 per cent of the Union's casualties were inflicted by the Confederate artillery. This deployed artillery section is protected by a group of artillerymen armed with rifled muskets; they would be used to defend the crew against enemy sniper fire.

(Opposite below) Just as musketry fire would envelop the battlefield with smoke, so too would the charges used by the artillery, each shot consuming 2.5lb (1.1kg) of black powder. For close protection the majority of the artillerymen were armed with a Model 1851 Colt Navy revolver, usually housed in a holster attached to their belt. They carried their personal equipment in a haversack over the shoulder, in addition to a cap pouch, cartridge pouch and wooden water canteen. The majority of the enlisted gunners, at least in the early stages of the war, wore the predominantly red forage cap, although as the war continued the standard grey forage cap was adopted, with red piping. Officers and non-commissioned officers would also have a Model 1833 US Foot Artillery Short Sword. These had brass handles and were encased in a metal scabbard with a brass rim and tip.

(Above) This Confederate artillery unit includes men with a cotton Havelock, used in this case for additional protection to the neck from shrapnel. Counter-battery fire, as experienced by these crews, was commonplace as battles usually began with an artillery exchange. These counter-battery fire engagements could last up to an hour and a half as the respective commanders surveyed the battlefield and looked for weaknesses or hesitancy in the opposition. The crews depicted wear a variety of red striped and plain trousers. Most of the men have stripped off their forage jackets and are operating with all of their accoutrements in place, hung around their shoulders by white cotton straps. An officer can be seen to the rear, having taken up a position in order to survey the affect of his battery's fire on the enemy. A non-commissioned officer, in this case a sergeant, directs the manning of the guns.

(Opposite) Often in enemy controlled territory the Confederate forces set up a series of observation or signal stations. Ideally, a chain of these would mark the army's line of supply and communication. The primary role was to observe the surrounding area and to signal by semaphore, using flags. The Confederate camp near Manassas Junction in 1861 was protected by a series of signal stations, one of which reported the intended Union flank attack. The signal stations could intercept by reading enemy messages; later a form of cipher was used, such as the one developed by Myer for the Union in 1863. The three men on signal watch would be positioned at the extremity of the Confederate camp, but within sight of the camp itself so that messages could be relayed.

(Left) The Confederate artilleryman in the centre of the picture wears a waterproof poncho over his standard-issue uniform. Confederate artillerymen were issued with overcoats and protective gear, though many of the coats were issued without capes: Union overcoats and waterproofs were highly prized by Confederate artillerymen. The men wear short shell jackets with predominantly black leather straps and belts. A white cotton strap is attached to a covered metal canteen on the artilleryman on the left of the picture. The artillery corporal on the far right holds a ramrod. His waterproof poncho has been tied and fixed over his left shoulder. His haversack with personal belongings is of civilian design.

(Opposite) Various seated officers and men. The seated man with the dark grey uniform is probably a second lieutenant. His webbing and equipment is underneath his jacket and he has a watch chain extending from a button of his waistcoat to a slit pocket. The rudimentary cooking frame would be carried by several of the men and one of the first duties at a stop would be to gather firewood in order to brew coffee and make hot food. The majority of the men would use metal or enamel-plated drinking vessels.

(Top Left) Established camps would have a rudimentary parade ground where the regiments would be inspected, usually at dawn or dusk. Officers and non-commissioned officers would check the men's equipment and their health, and check rosters. The Stars and Bars would flutter above the parade ground at the centre of the camp, acting as a muster point or rallying point in times of emergency.

(Left) These two Confederate officers around a campfire illustrate the individuality of the uniforms adopted by officers of various ranks. The individual standing is a first lieutenant with an Austrian-knot design on his frock coat. He wears brown boots with socks tied with a leather strap. Around his waist is a revolver holster, a cartridge pouch and a cap pouch. He has a cummerbund of a red material tied around his waist and he appears to be wearing a black waistcoat and a white collarless shirt with the top button fastened. His fellow officer has a shorter jacket with epaulettes and appears to be a second lieutenant, as he has an Austrian-knot design on his left sleeve. This officer has opted for black boots and socks. Both men wear dark blue trousers.

Camp Life

P ART of a recruit's rough and ready training was to teach him how to live outdoors. If the men were lucky and they were in an established camp, then it was likely that they would have tents, bivouacs or, during the winter months, log-built dugouts. The men would be undergoing constant training, regardless of their length of service. Both the Union and the Confederacy, by 1862, had instituted a three-year service period for volunteers. After this period increasing numbers of conscripts filled the ranks. It would take a man between three and twelve months to become accustomed to his new way of life; a year after this the man could be considered to be a veteran. All of the regiments had a mixture of veteran campaigners and newly inducted recruits.

Living in the open, the men would have to ration themselves and ensure that they had sufficient food stocks to last them into the immediate future. The provisioning of units often came second to ensuring that they had sufficient arms and ammunition

to fight a battle. The men cooked in the open, not knowing from one day to the next whether they were in an established long-term camp or whether this would be a temporary stop. Sanitary conditions were extremely poor. Men would routinely use the same water source for drinking water, bathing and disposing of their own and the camp's waste products. At any one time a large number of the men would be stricken with a variety of fevers, particularly in the deeper southern states where malaria, dysentery and typhoid were rife.

When the army marched it was accompanied by a host of camp followers. A certain percentage of women – wives of enlisted men, officers and non-commissioned officers – would be allowed to remain with the regiment and carry out cooking duties and attending to the wounded.

Journalists, representatives from the state government and other civilians accompanied their state regiments for the purposes of reporting or simply to experience army life.

(Above) Morale was vitally important for both armies. Many of the men were hundreds of miles from home, living in harsh and dangerous conditions. The men were encouraged to make their own entertainment, particularly after dusk, where for an hour or so the men would entertain one another with music, storytelling and even dancing. Alcohol was relatively rare, although raw whiskey and gin were the favoured drinks, if they could be acquired.

(Opposite) Infantry non-commissioned officers were at the hub of camp life. They would direct the men to gather firewood, establish the tenting positions and forage in the local area to supplement their meagre rations. These NCOs are depicted as wearing a variety of grey tunics, from dark to light. Two wear darker trousers while the third, a corporal, has mid-blue jean-style trousers. The corporal to the rear has boots, and his trousers are tucked into his socks. The other two men appear to have regular-issue shoes.

(Right) This Confederate fifer would not only have daytime duties at the head of the regiment or alongside the drummer boys, but would also be expected to provide stirring and patriotic music during the battles. In camp, fifers provided official or impromptu performances as one of the only means of entertainment for the troops.

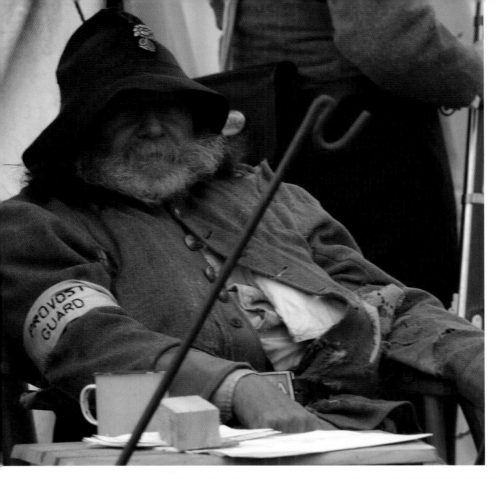

(Left) The provost guard was established to discipline the largely untrained soldiers in the Confederate ranks. They were the watchdogs of the camp, effectively the official military police of the time. The provost guard tended to be older men beyond normal combat age and were often detailed to protect railroad depots, food stores and munitions. They would instil discipline and seek to prevent desertion, or fights breaking out between regiments. This provost guard wears a simple armband that denotes his military title. To all intents and purposes he is armed in exactly the same way as a regular infantryman. In this case he wears a ragged butternut-grey jacket and trousers and has a floppy broad-brimmed hat. The badge appears to denote that he is from North Carolina.

(Right) This Confederate is cooking his bacon using a drum-shaped stove. He wears long cavalry-style boots, into which he has tucked his mid-blue trousers that are held up by a pair of white cotton braces. He wears a loose-fitting four-button shirt and has a civilian-style forage cap in black.

(Opposite) These enlisted men are preparing a breakfast. The men carried corn, oats and other non-perishable items. The food would need to be supplemented by whatever they could find en route. As the war progressed the provisioning of the Confederate Army became a more acute problem: often, large bodies of Confederate troops were cut off in enemy-held territory and simply had to fend for themselves. The enlisted man in the foreground wears a rough homespun jacket and light-coloured trousers. The bulk of his equipment and strapping is black, but he wears the familiar cotton strap around his left shoulder attached to his canteen.

(Right) This Confederate veteran has a short, cadet-grey shell jacket over a civilian black and white check shirt. His trousers appear to be of similar material and he carries a brown cartridge pouch on a black belt with a round Eastern Theatre pattern buckle. He has slung his haversack over his left shoulder and on his right he has his canteen, over which is a waterproof poncho. His kepi is of standard issue with a brass bugle design, black strap and black leather peak.

(Opposite) Many of the men were devout Christians. Here we see a mixed group of officers and men attending a prayer meeting prior to battle. The officer in the foreground has dark trousers laced at the back and a light butternut shell jacket. He carries a Model 1840 cavalry sabre in a blackened metal scabbard with brass mounts. His percussion-cap pouch is in brown leather, resembling the standard southern-made cap box, with a central fastening strap. His haversack is also of brown leather and his canteen is of the southern-made, tin-drum-style pattern.

(Left) Many thousands of African Americans served alongside white men in the regiments. Others acted as uniformed or civilian-clothed servants and labourers. This man wears a brown uniform with a grey-blue collar. He may well be part of a labour battalion: these men were normally assigned to the construction of fortifications and gun emplacements, and would be used to clear trees and lines of fire for artillery, to bring up supplies and to carry out a wide variety of camp duties. Despite the Confederacy's reliance on slavery, by 1865 the Confederate Government had authorized the wholesale recruitment of able-bodied African Americans into the army in exchange for compensation to their owners and freedom for the men. By this stage of the war, however, despite the fact that several thousand African Americans were already unofficially serving, the war was too close to its conclusion for the change in policy to have any marked effect.

(Below) Official army supply was coupled to civilian entrepreneurs in providing the men in the field with additional equipment, from hurricane lamps to pots and pans and from axes to hides and leather.

(Opposite) These two men representing either state visitors or journalists wear typical civilian clothing of the period. Note how similar the military dress is in style to its civilian counterpart. The man on the left is wearing a long, frock-coat-style jacket, while the man on the right is wearing a shorter, shell-type civilian version of the jacket. Both men wear hats that could quite conceivably have been found on the heads of Confederate infantrymen.

Towards the end of the war, with inflation raging in the south, even the simplest items could cost several dollars and were well beyond the means of most enlisted men, who had probably not been paid for several months.

(Above) A man depicting either a Confederate civilian, or an officer or enlisted man in his civilian clothes. Any opportunity to return to a semblance of normality was grasped at by the men. This individual wears a check shirt with a rounded white collar. He wears a knotted green silk cravat and his pipe is a typical wealthier man's pattern of the period. His hat is a broad-brimmed felt design with a rigid brim, and has a black silk headband.

(Left) This photograph represents the archetypal image of the dashing Confederate cavalier and his adoring belle. Women such as Belle Boyd provided more than companionship for the Confederates. Boyd was born in Martinsburg, Virginia and constantly provided information to Stonewall Jackson; she later served as a scout for Mosby's guerrillas. She was arrested on several occasions by Union forces and in 1864 she fled to England with letters to Confederate sympathisers from President Jefferson Davis. Belle Boyd was not to marry a dashing Confederate cavalryman but in fact married a Union sailor and

had a second career as an actress and a third one as a lecturer. She died in Wisconsin in 1900.

(Opposite) A Confederate surgeon leading a wounded infantryman away from the battle line. He wears standard-issue trousers and boots, a white shirt and a grey waistcoat with a white cotton back. He has a black cravat around his neck and from his shoulders hang a water bottle and a haversack containing dressings; from his waist belt hangs a leather pouch containing surgical equipment, including knives and scissors. He wears a light blue cap with a leather strap and brim. Surgeons were ill equipped to deal with the fractures caused by Minié bullets and were powerless to stop gangrene. They were overwhelmed during and after a battle, and many thousands of men died before they even received any medical attention. A wounded man had a reasonable chance of survival, assuming that he survived loss of blood and dehydration. Nearly three quarters of wounds were to the limbs and often the only solution was amputation.

(Above) A female camp follower, probably the wife of a non-commissioned officer or an officer, attends a campfire. Her striped dress is full length with buttons to the front. The dress has puffed sleeves and a single button at the cuff. Over her dress she wears a rough cloth pinafore and her hair is tied back in a bun, covered by a net.

(Left) A group of female civilians attached to an army camp. They wear a variety of period costumes and the children wear lace bonnets. Note the layers of clothing. A long under-dress would be worn, which would then be covered by a long-sleeved garment, almost resembling a petticoat. Over the top of this would be worn a second dress. Regardless of the rank of their husbands or fathers, these women would be acutely aware of the fact that the average number of men killed, wounded or missing could be anything from 7 to 27 per cent in a single engagement.

(Opposite) A Confederate enlisted man in a long frock jacket in cadet grey and matching trousers is seen here on his wedding day. Many Confederate wives had very little time to experience the joys of marriage with their husbands: many thousands would never see their husbands again. The bride wears a typical wedding dress of the period, with a long veil. Under her skirts are hoops attached to a petticoat that were designed to give a fuller shape to the skirt of the dress.

Acknowledgements

The authors are indebted to the American Civil War Society and the innumerable photographers who provided these posed shots from a variety of public and private events during several re-enactment campaign seasons. Photographs are drawn from events at Cornbury Park, Weston Park and Steam, Strife and Secession. Individual photographers include Geoff Buxton, Ian Dunning of the Defence School of Photography and Mike McCormac. Thanks also go to the countless numbers of ACWS members for agreeing to be featured in this book.

More wealthy southern women. These women are likely to be the wives or daughters of Confederate officers. If their husbands or fathers fell in battle there was a chance, if the man was wealthy enough, that his body would be embalmed and returned to them. Most of the casualties, on the other hand, were buried in shallow graves or left where they fell. Friends in the regiment might leave an improvised marker on the gravesite, but for many women the bodies of their fallen family members were never discovered or identified.